Oskee in Illini Land:
Memoirs of a Small Canine on a Large College Campus

written by Joanne Holzgrafe
photographs by Holly Smith

*To The Corners
Thank goodness
I learned to type—
Go Illini!
Joanne*

oskee

All photographs by Holly Birch Photography (www.hollybirchphotography.com), except where noted. Grateful acknowledgment to the Board of Trustees of the University of Illinois for use of the song lyrics.

Copyright © 2009 by Joanne C. Holzgrafe
Little White Dog Press
P.O. Box 422
Quincy, IL 62306
www.oskeesbook.com

All rights reserved. No part of this book may be reproduced in any form, without permission in writing from the author.

ISBN 978-1-61584-551-4

Printed in the USA by JK Creative Printers, Quincy, Illinois

Dedicated To
Oskee

"He is your friend, your partner, your defender, your dog.
You are his life, his love, his leader.
He will be yours, faithful and true, to the last beat of his heart.
You owe it to him to be worthy of such devotion."
Unknown author

Special thanks to the ladies of 4-H House
who let me be a Mom for two special years,
to Kayla Rassi Hedrick for her time and talent in editing,
and to my friends and family for their support.

Allow me to begin my memories of a wonderful period in my life by defining a few terms.

1) My name is Oskee like in Wow Wow. If you are an Illini, you know what I mean.

2) I call the person who walks me, feeds me and makes me feel like the luckiest dog alive PetMom.

3) Sometimes dogs are put in a car and taken on long rides to unknown and even final destinations. I was put in a car and taken on a long ride to live in a sorority with fifty-five women on the University of Illinois campus. Winning the dog lottery is the only way to explain it.

Come down to the ground level with me and I will give you my perspective of what life was like on campus.

Daybreak would arrive and my first duty of the day was to take PetMom on a "business trip." My favorite destination was the Quad. It was quiet there early in the morning. Hearing the Altgeld chimes break through the silence to announce the time of day made me happy and my little paws felt good as I bounced across the grass.

Illinois Loyalty

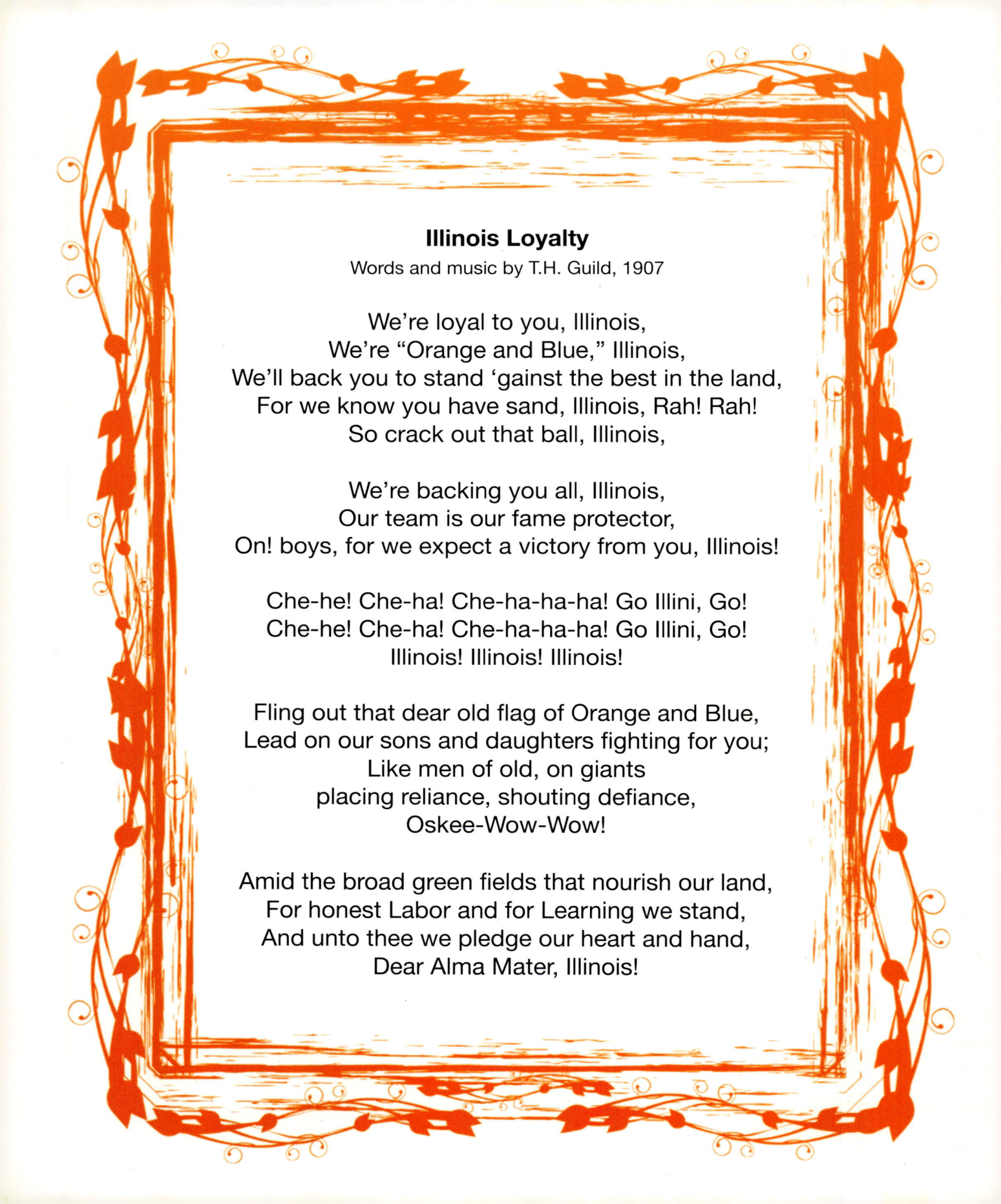

Words and music by T.H. Guild, 1907

We're loyal to you, Illinois,
We're "Orange and Blue," Illinois,
We'll back you to stand 'gainst the best in the land,
For we know you have sand, Illinois, Rah! Rah!
So crack out that ball, Illinois,

We're backing you all, Illinois,
Our team is our fame protector,
On! boys, for we expect a victory from you, Illinois!

Che-he! Che-ha! Che-ha-ha-ha! Go Illini, Go!
Che-he! Che-ha! Che-ha-ha-ha! Go Illini, Go!
Illinois! Illinois! Illinois!

Fling out that dear old flag of Orange and Blue,
Lead on our sons and daughters fighting for you;
Like men of old, on giants
placing reliance, shouting defiance,
Oskee-Wow-Wow!

Amid the broad green fields that nourish our land,
For honest Labor and for Learning we stand,
And unto thee we pledge our heart and hand,
Dear Alma Mater, Illinois!

Many times upon returning home, however, PetMom carried me into the house and put me in her bathtub, washing off the sand that collected on my feet. We always thought it had something to do with that "we know you have sand" line in the song. It was messy.

One day PetMom took me to the Post Office that is located inside Altgeld Hall. That beautiful building is one of the oldest on campus. She put me in her bag and told me to be very quiet. I do not know if it was out of respect for the building or if I was being smuggled inside.

Often a young lady would ask PetMom if she could pet me because she missed her dog. I became a stand-in for pooches all over the world, from beagles to retrievers, and loved every minute of it… a dirty job, but somedoggy had to do it.

There are some beautiful buildings on campus and even though I had a personal relationship with all the trash bins and lampposts, I was aware of those big and important halls of learning.

PetMom and I would climb the steps of Foellinger Auditorium and enjoy the view across the Quad looking toward the Illini Union. If we got there at noon, we could hear the Altgeld chimes play Illinois Loyalty.

I especially enjoyed walking by the Child Development Lab when the little kids were playing outside. My ears would perk up when I heard students practicing their pianos and other instruments in the Smith Music Hall.

Occasionally we would walk through Illini Grove. Students went there to have cookouts and play touch football. The grills and tables made a great place to have a picnic. One day as we strolled through the leaves, I found a yummy treasure—a charred hamburger. I grabbed it. PetMom grabbed it. I won.

She was concerned that it would re-emerge so we went for an extra long walk. We traveled all the way to the Assembly Hall, across the street to Memorial Stadium, past the Six Pack, back to Allen Hall and Lincoln Avenue Residence Hall, then home. After walking off the burger, my little legs were tired but my nose never forgot to hit the ground when jaunting through Illini Grove.

The side of campus with Assembly Hall and Memorial Stadium kept me in touch with my animal brethren when the wind was blowing from the direction of the South Farms. Most of the students did not enjoy that scent, but it let me know that I had four-legged friends in close proximity.

I loved walking over to the football stadium on game day. The band would play Oskee Wow Wow—my personal favorite—and the students and fans would wear orange. They would yell things like "Go Illini," "I-L-L" and "I-N-I!" to get our team to score points and win. I wonder what would happen if they shouted, "roll over" or "play dead" to the other team.

Oskee Wow Wow

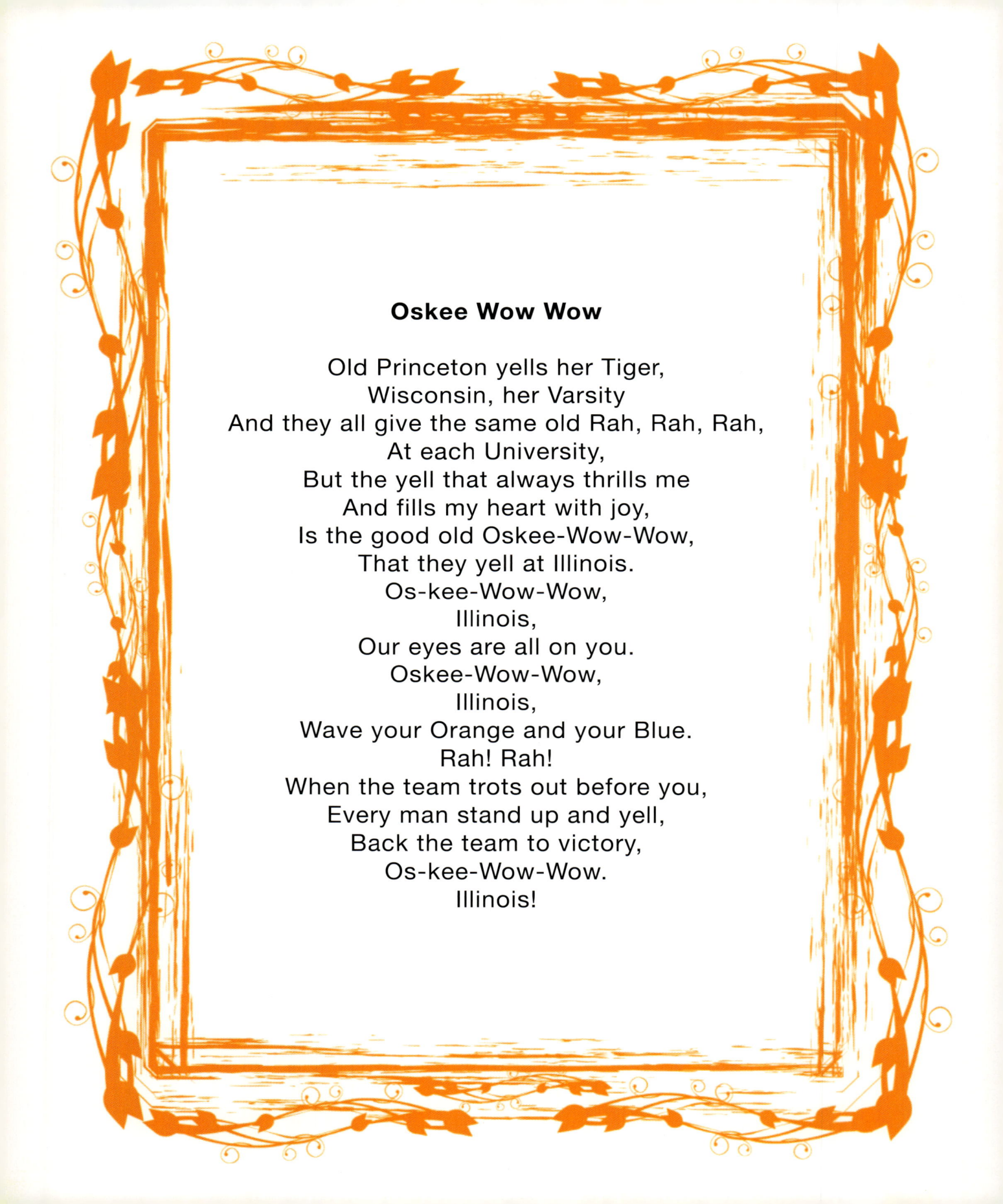

Old Princeton yells her Tiger,
Wisconsin, her Varsity
And they all give the same old Rah, Rah, Rah,
At each University,
But the yell that always thrills me
And fills my heart with joy,
Is the good old Oskee-Wow-Wow,
That they yell at Illinois.
Os-kee-Wow-Wow,
Illinois,
Our eyes are all on you.
Oskee-Wow-Wow,
Illinois,
Wave your Orange and your Blue.
Rah! Rah!
When the team trots out before you,
Every man stand up and yell,
Back the team to victory,
Os-kee-Wow-Wow.
Illinois!

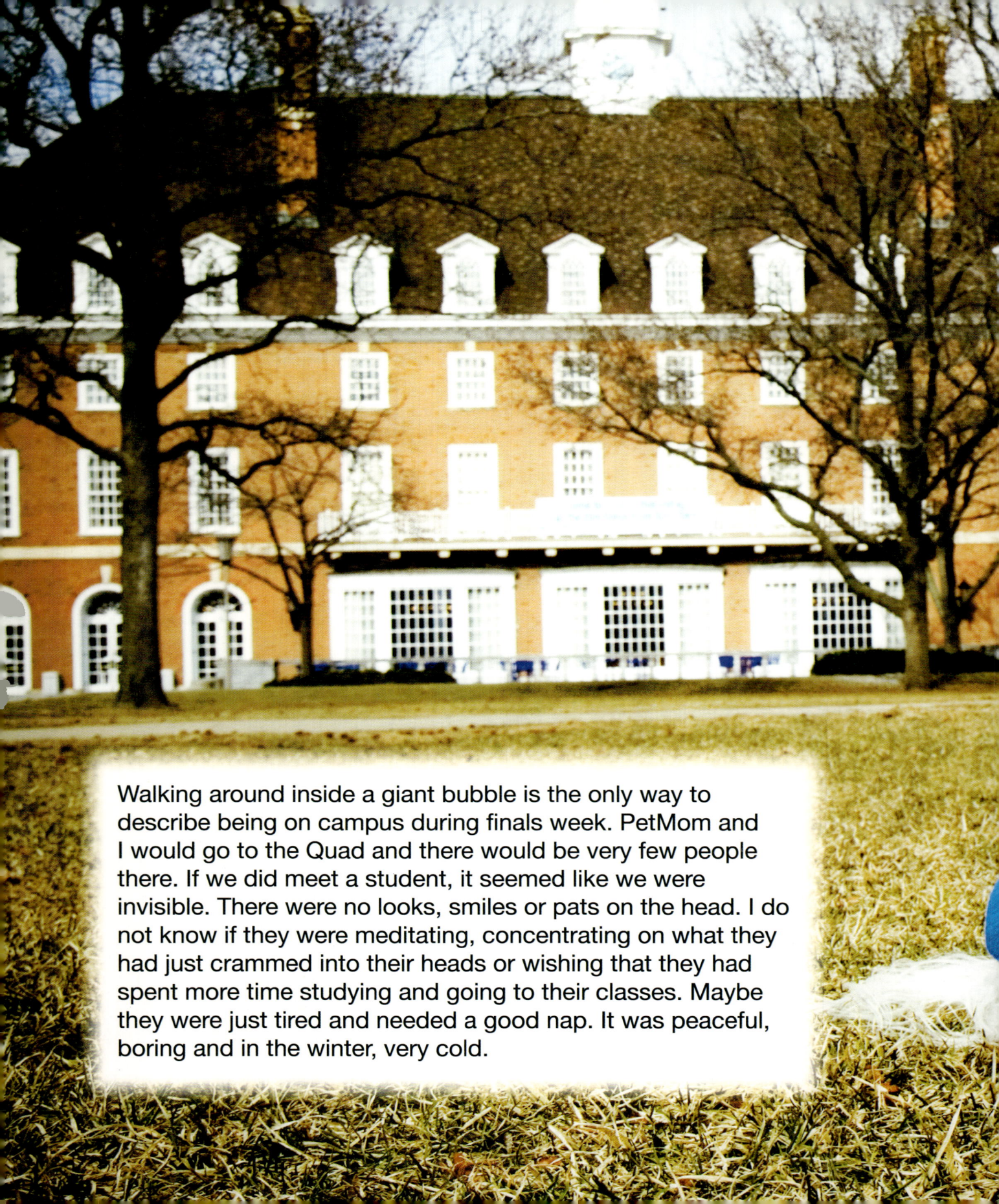

Walking around inside a giant bubble is the only way to describe being on campus during finals week. PetMom and I would go to the Quad and there would be very few people there. If we did meet a student, it seemed like we were invisible. There were no looks, smiles or pats on the head. I do not know if they were meditating, concentrating on what they had just crammed into their heads or wishing that they had spent more time studying and going to their classes. Maybe they were just tired and needed a good nap. It was peaceful, boring and in the winter, very cold.

Our campus is located in the middle of lots of flat farmland; and when the north wind whips across campus, it is blustery. An essential for every student is a warm coat. How do you like mine?

One of the worst days of my life in Illini Land was a beautiful spring afternoon when we were strolling down Lincoln Avenue. I wanted to check out a tree. My leash was retractable and I stretched it across the grass. About the same time, a bicycle rode over the grass, too. I turned back and... BOOM! I GOT SCHWINNED (which is how students refer to being run over by a bicycle)!

I have never felt so bad or been so scared. PetMom was afraid I had a broken back. I wondered if she would take me across the street to McKinley Student Health Center or do the right thing and go the extra mile to the Veterinary School. However, I think that part about an Illini "having sand" kicked in and I shook it off. PetMom carried me home, put me down and I escaped to the off-limits dining room to sniff for crumbs under the tables. She knew I was going to be all right. It was a memorable day. I now know why she always told the new students not to walk on those bicycle paths that crisscross campus.

I do not care if you are country, urban or suburban, you have to love the uniqueness of the Morrow Plots. Not many campuses have a real live cornfield that grows in the midst of the state seat of higher learning.
It is the oldest agricultural experimental plot in the western hemisphere and makes our campus unique. I loved walking around it and seeing the corn go from green to gone in the fall.

PetMom says there is a song that tells why I could walk on top of the neighboring Undergraduate Library and why it was believed to be under the ground so it would not shade that corn.

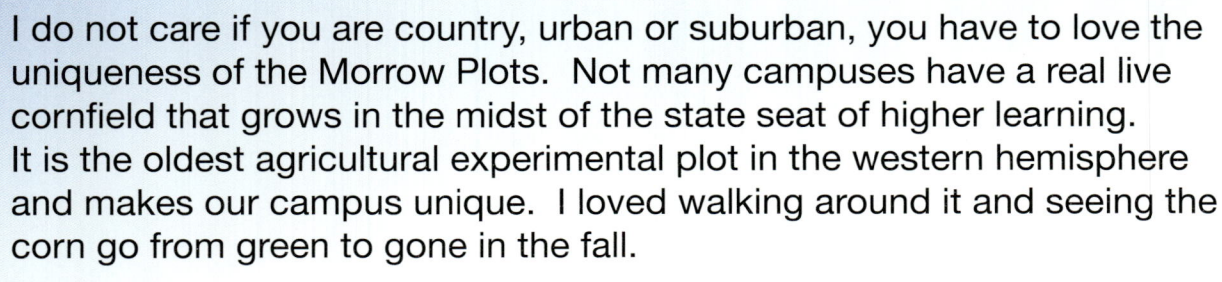

As I wrap up this account of my life at the University of Illinois in Urbana-Champaign, I have saved the most awesome sight until last.

When the evenings were nice, especially in the spring and fall, PetMom and I would walk across campus to see that lady—the one at Green and Wright—the Alma Mater. With the lights on her, she had a special glow and an all-knowing smile on her face. I wondered if it was because she was proud to be there or if she knew the secrets of all who passed by her and even ventured high enough to climb into her chair.

I always gave her a big "bark out" for standing tall as she watches students come and go to class and having pictures taken before her, but never once taking a break to sit and stay. It must be that "sand" thing again. She makes even a little ten-pound ball of fluff like me proud to have been there.

Go Illini and Oskee Wow Wow!

Hail to the Orange

Hail to the Orange,
Hail to the Blue,
Hail Alma Mater,
Ever so true!
We love no other
So let our motto be
Victory, Illinois! Varsity!

I have told you my memories of being at the University of Illinois. Here is a place for you to write yours:

Thanks, Illinois!

I had a ball!

www.oskeesbook.com

Joanne Holzgrafe, "PetMom," graduated from the University of Illinois in 1970 with a degree in Child Development and MEd in Elementary Education. In 2002, she went back to campus to serve as House Director at 4-H House. She served her former campus home until 2005. She and Oskee now reside in Quincy, Illinois.
Photo courtesy of Memory Lane Photography, Scott Christenson

Holly Birch Smith is the owner of Holly Birch Photography and a 2003 graduate of the University of Illinois. She lived at 4-H House when Joanne came to be the House Director. Holly and her husband Aaron live with their two dogs, Paisley & Sophie, in Urbana, Illinois.
Photo courtesy of Sweet Pea Photography, Allyson Sanborn

Hey, photo lady! Can I go now?